SPACE FLIGHT ADVENTURES AND DISASTERS

PIONEERING ASTRONAUT SALLY RIDE

A MYREPORTLINKS.COM BOOK

HENRY M. HOLDEN

MyReportLinks.com Books
an imprint of
 Enslow Publishers, Inc.
Box 398, 40 Industrial Road
Berkeley Heights, NJ 07922
USA

MyReportLinks.com Books, an imprint of Enslow Publishers, Inc. MyReportLinks®
is a registered trademark of Enslow Publishers, Inc.

Library of Congress Cataloging-in-Publication Data

Holden, Henry M.
  Pioneering astronaut Sally Ride / Henry M. Holden.
    p. cm. — (Space flight adventures and disasters)
Summary: A biography of Sally Ride, who in 1983 became the first
American woman to travel in space.
Includes bibliographical references and index.
  ISBN 0-7660-5169-2
  1. Ride, Sally—Juvenile literature. 2. Women astronauts—United
States—Biography—Juvenile literature. 3. Astronauts—United
States—Biography—Juvenile literature. [1. Ride, Sally. 2. Astronauts.
3. Women—Biography.] I. Title. II. Series.
  TL789.85.R53H64 2004
  629.45'0092—dc22

                           2003016491

Printed in the United States of America

10 9 8 7 6 5 4 3 2 1

To Our Readers:
Through the purchase of this book, you and your library gain access to the Report Links that specifically back
up this book.
The Publisher will provide access to the Report Links that back up this book and will keep these Report Links
up to date on **www.myreportlinks.com** for three years from the book's first publication date.
We have done our best to make sure all Internet addresses in this book were active and appropriate when we
went to press. However, the author and the Publisher have no control over, and assume no liability for, the
material available on those Internet sites or on other Web sites they may link to.
The usage of the MyReportLinks.com Books Web site is subject to the terms and conditions stated on the
Usage Policy Statement on **www.myreportlinks.com**.
A password may be required to access the Report Links that back up this book. The password is found on the
bottom of page 4 of this book.
Any comments or suggestions can be sent by e-mail to comments@myreportlinks.com or to the address on
the back cover.

Photo Credits: © 2003 Mark Wade, p. 40; © 2003 Microsoft Corporation, p. 20; Copyright
Imaginary Lines, Inc., 2003–2004, p. 38 MyReportLinks.com Books, p. 4; National Aeronautics and
Space Administration (NASA), pp. 3, 10, 12, 13, 14, 19, 23, 24, 26, 29, 31, 35, 36, 39, 41, 42;
Photos.com, p. 1; Smithsonian Institution, pp. 16, 22, 33.

Cover Photo: NASA

Cover Description: Sally Ride aboard the space shuttle *Challenger*.

Contents

MyReportLinks.com Books
Great Books, Great Links, Great for Research!

The Report Links listed on the following four pages can save you hours of research time by **instantly** bringing you to the best Web sites relating to your report topic.

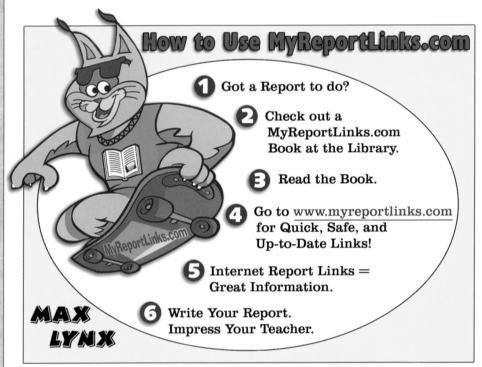

How to Use MyReportLinks.com

1 Got a Report to do?

2 Check out a MyReportLinks.com Book at the Library.

3 Read the Book.

4 Go to www.myreportlinks.com for Quick, Safe, and Up-to-Date Links!

5 Internet Report Links = Great Information.

6 Write Your Report. Impress Your Teacher.

MAX LYNX

The pre-evaluated Web sites are your links to source documents, photographs, illustrations, and maps. They also provide links to dozens—even hundreds—of Web sites about your report subject.

MyReportLinks.com Books and the MyReportLinks.com Web site save you time and make report writing easier than ever!

Please see "To Our Readers" on the copyright page for important information about this book, the MyReportLinks.com Web site, and the Report Links that back up this book. Please enter **FSR1887** if asked for a password.

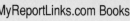

Report Links

The Internet sites described below can be accessed at http://www.myreportlinks.com

*EDITOR'S CHOICE

▶**Biographical Data: Sally K. Ride**
The biographical profile of Sally Ride from the Lyndon B. Johnson Space Center. Learn about her education, NASA experience, and more.

*EDITOR'S CHOICE

▶**STS-7**
With her participation in the *Challenger* STS-7 mission, Sally Ride became the first American woman in space. Read about this historic flight.

*EDITOR'S CHOICE

▶**Dr. Sally Ride: First American Woman in Space**
This page, maintained by the National Women's History Museum, gives a short biography of Sally Ride and tells of her impact on the worlds of science and space technology.

*EDITOR'S CHOICE

▶**Tereshkova, Valentina**
While Sally Ride was the first American woman in space, Russian cosmonaut Valentina Tereshkova has the honor of being the first-ever woman to venture into space. Learn a bit about her at this Web site.

*EDITOR'S CHOICE

▶**NASA**
The National Aeronautics and Space Administration (NASA) home page provides all sorts of information about the world of science and space technology. Special sections for young people and students lead to interesting articles, activities, and games.

*EDITOR'S CHOICE

▶**Women of Space**
This site gives pictures and biographies of women who have flown in space. It includes information about their missions and how many days they have spent in space.

Report Links

**The Internet sites described below can be accessed at
http://www.myreportlinks.com**

▶ **The Astronaut Connection**

At this comprehensive site, you can learn all about space travel and technology: from biographies of famous astronauts to descriptions of different space vehicles. Also included is a time line of historic events in space exploration.

▶ **Biographical Data: Frederick H. (Rick) Hauck**

Frederick H. Hauck was the pilot on Sally Ride's first mission to space. On this site, you can learn about his NASA experience and facts about his life.

▶ **Biographical Data: John M. Fabian**

On Sally Ride's first mission aboard the *Challenger*, John M. Fabian was one of the mission specialists. This site provides a brief biography of this astronaut.

▶ **Biographical Data: Norman E. Thagard**

On this site, you can read a brief biography of Norman E. Thagard. He was one of the mission specialists aboard Sally Ride's first mission to space.

▶ **Biographical Data: Robert L. Crippen**

Robert Crippen was the commander of the *Challenger* in 1983 when Sally Ride made her historic flight. Learn about this amazing astronaut on this Web site.

▶ **Challenger Center: 51-L Crew**

Less than three years after Sally Ride's voyage aboard the Space Shuttle *Challenger*, seven astronauts lost their lives aboard the same ship. Learn about these heroic astronauts by clicking on their names and downloading their bios.

▶ **Challenging the Space Frontier: Sally Ride Interview**

In this extensive interview, Sally Ride answers all kinds of questions from students, such as how it felt to be the first American woman in space, and what space food tastes like.

▶ *Columbia* **Tragedy Brings Together World of Mourners**

In February 2003, space exploration received a terrible blow when the Space Shuttle *Columbia* broke up on reentry into Earth's atmosphere. This article gives information on this tragic event. Ride was one of the people appointed to investigate the accident.

Any comments? Contact us: **comments@myreportlinks.com**

Report Links

The Internet sites described below can be accessed at http://www.myreportlinks.com

▶ **Female First Flights**

Learn about some of the most famous women in air and space history, including Amelia Earhart and Sally Ride, and the impact each made on the world. Click on these women's names to learn some of their biographical information.

▶ **History Time Lines**

These comprehensive time lines highlight the history of NASA and space exploration for nearly the past one hundred years. Special features include a chronology of major events, a "This Month in Space History" section, and more.

▶ **How Space Shuttles Work**

Have you ever wondered how space shuttles are able to orbit Earth, or how they can support the lives of their crews while in space? Learn all about space shuttles at this comprehensive site. Includes a table of contents for easy site navigation.

▶ **How to Go to Space: How Rockets Work**

When space shuttles take off from the ground, they rely on rockets to propel them high above Earth and into space. Learn how rockets work at this Web site.

▶ **Imaginary Lines**

Imaginary Lines is a company that Sally Ride founded to encourage girls to become interested in science and technology. On its official Web site, learn about the company and the programs that it offers.

▶ **ISS EarthKAM**

In order to strengthen ties between space science and education, Sally Ride developed EarthKAM. At the organization's Web site, you can learn about the EarthKAM program, look at pictures taken from space, read related articles, and more.

▶ **Kennedy Space Center**

Here, you can visit the Kennedy Space Center in Cape Canaveral, Florida, where many space shuttles are launched. Updates about future launches, links to articles, and historical information about the space program are included here.

▶ **KidsAstronomy.com**

Before traveling into space, it is important to know a few things about astronomy. This site explains the solar system, the universe, space travel, and more.

The Internet sites described below can be accessed at
http://www.myreportlinks.com

▶**Living in Space**

Have you ever wondered how astronauts were able to live and work in zero gravity? Learn how at this site.

▶*Mercury 13*—**The Women of the Mercury Era**

More than twenty years before Sally Ride's historic flight, thirteen talented women had passed the necessary requirements to join NASA and become astronauts, but they never got the chance to fly to space. Find out about the *Mercury 13* at this Web site.

▶**NASA Kids**

This site is loaded with articles, features, and games that can help kids learn more about space. It includes biographies of famous scientists, facts about space and technology, interviews, and more.

▶**National Air and Space Museum**

At this site you can explore the National Air and Space Museum's numerous exhibits about air and space exploration, as well as technology and research. View pictures, take virtual tours, and more.

▶**Sally Ride is Leaving NASA After Making Major Contributions**

This article appeared in the *Houston Chronicle* in 1987 when Sally Ride left NASA to take a position at Stanford University. Learn about her life after the astronaut program, contributions to the world of space travel, and her legacy.

▶**Space Academy: What is Microgravity?**

As part of her training to become an astronaut, Sally Ride had to experience what it feels like to live without gravity. Find out about this interesting experiment.

▶**spaceKids**

Learn about space travel and exploration at this Web site. Games, movies, and pictures make it interesting. Post a question at the "Ask the Experts" section, and read articles on related topics.

▶**Two Decades Later, Sally Ride's Mission Continues**

June 2003 marked the twentieth anniversary of Sally Ride's historic flight into space. This article reflects on the past twenty years of space exploration and tells about Sally Ride's life and achievements.

Sally Ride Facts

1951—*May 26:* Born in a suburb of Los Angeles, California.

1968—Graduates from Westlake High School for Girls.

1973—Graduates from Stanford University with a Bachelor of Science in Physics and a Bachelor of Arts in English.

1975—Receives Master of Science degree in Physics from Stanford University.

1978—*Jan. 16:* Selected by NASA for astronaut training.
—Receives doctorate degree in physics from Stanford University.

1982–87—Married to astronaut Steven Hawley.

1983—*June 18:* Flies her first mission to space, Mission STS-7, aboard the space shuttle *Challenger.*
—*June 24:* Returns safely from Mission STS-7.

1984—*Oct. 5:* Flies her second mission to space, Mission STS-41G, aboard the space shuttle *Challenger.*
—*Oct. 13:* Returns safely from Mission STS-41G.
—Wins Jefferson Award for Public Service.

1986—*Jan. to June:* Serves as a member of the presidential commission investigating the cause of the space shuttle *Challenger* accident.
—Publishes a book for young people titled, *To Space and Back.*

1988—Inducted into National Women's Hall of Fame.

1989–2004—Chief of Space Institute, University of California, San Diego.

1992—Publishes a book for young people titled, *The Mystery of Mars.*

2003—Publishes a book for young people titled, *Exploring Our Solar System.*

Chapter 1

GO FOR LAUNCH

Millions of people were watching on television. Thousands more were sitting along Florida's sandy beaches. They were there to see the launch of the space shuttle *Challenger*. However, they also were there to cheer on Sally Ride, as she would try to become the first American woman to fly into space.

After several delays, *Challenger* STS-7, the seventh shuttle mission, was ready to go. On June 18, 1983, the crew ate a hearty breakfast of steak and eggs. Then they

▲ The crew of Challenger's seventh mission: (left to right) Sally Ride, John Fabian, Norman Thagard, Robert Crippen, and Frederick Hauck.

rode together in a van to the launchpad. The first rays of the morning sun were coloring the sky in shades of orange.

Ride and the others looked up at the two thousand tons of rocket and spacecraft. It towered almost two hundred feet (61 meters) into the air. This was going to be an exciting ride.

An elevator took the crew up to the nose of the shuttle. Technicians checked the crew's flight suits and helped them put on their helmets. The helmet provides oxygen and communications with Mission Control. Sally Ride and the other crew members climbed through a small hatch to board *Challenger*. They were lying on their backs in seats that faced the nose of the shuttle. From that position, it is hard to see out the windows. They strapped into their seats and got ready for the launch. The hatch closed on *Challenger*. Sally Ride, Commander Robert L. Crippen, Pilot Captain Frederick H. Hauck, and mission specialists Colonel John M. Fabian and Dr. Norman E. Thagard were sealed in the spacecraft. This was the first mission with a five-person crew.

Sally Ride knew much of the world was watching. She also knew that her husband, Steven Hawley, (also an astronaut) her parents, and sister were watching from a special room at the launch site.

At T-minus zero seconds in the countdown, the two white solid fuel rocket boosters ignited. These were attached to each side of the huge external fuel tank. Each of the boosters carried more than one million pounds (453,592 kilograms) of solid fuel. They helped the main engines lift the shuttle and accelerate it to more than 2,800 miles per hour (4,506 kilometers per hour).

Lift Off! *Challenger* roared off the launchpad. This was *Challenger's* second mission. At age thirty-two, Sally Ride

▲ Challenger *carried Sally Ride on her first mission. Liftoff occurred at 7:33:00 AM EDT on June 18, 1983. The crew would remain in space for a total of six days, two hours, twenty-three minutes, and fifty-nine seconds.*

was the youngest American, and the first American woman, to be launched into orbit. Sally Ride was making history.

The vehicle was moving at one hundred miles per hour by the time it cleared the tower. The liftoff pushed Sally Ride and the other astronauts into their seats. They felt three times their body weight pressing down on them. The astronauts' heart rates, which are normally around eighty-five beats per minute, would rise to over one hundred beats per minute. Spectators on the beaches were holding posters reading "Ride Sally, Ride." This was a popular slogan from the famous song, "Mustang Sally," written by Wilson Pickett.

Two minutes later, Ride and the others were traveling at almost 17,500 miles per hour (28,163 kilometers per hour). They were going nearly five miles a second.

As a child, Ride was interested in the stars and planets. She never dreamed she would one day fly in space. Fifty-one years earlier, Amelia Earhart flew alone across the Atlantic Ocean. Perhaps not since then did the world pay such attention to a woman pilot.

Sally Ride floats next to the ▶ airlock hatch aboard the space shuttle Challenger.

Chapter 2

GROWING UP

Sally Kristen Ride was born in a Los Angeles, California, suburb, on May 26, 1951. Her father, Dr. Dale Ride, was a professor of political science. Her mother, Joyce, stayed at home. Neither of her parents had much of an interest in math or science.[1] Her younger sister, Karen, eventually became a Presbyterian minister.

When Sally was growing up, it was assumed that most little girls would try to become nurses, teachers, or stay-at-home mothers when they got older. Most parents did not

▲ On February 20, 1962, John Glenn became the first American to orbit the earth. Sally Ride was only ten years old at the time. Yet, she was inspired by Glenn's journey.

encourage their daughters to explore other fields. Sally's parents were different. They let Sally and her sister try anything that interested them. "We pursued a careful hands-off policy when the girls were growing up," said her mother, "and molding them into an astronaut and a minister is certainly something we never thought about."[2] They did "make sure I studied and brought home the right kind of grades," Sally said.[3]

Sally liked to read, especially mysteries and science fiction. "I read all the Nancy Drew books. I read all the Danny Dunn books. . . . One was *Danny Dunn and the Anti-Gravity Paint*."[4] These were popular mystery books of the time.

Many changes were taking place in the field of space exploration at this time. In 1957, the Soviet Union launched *Sputnik 1*, the first artificial satellite to orbit Earth. The following year the United States created the National Aeronautics and Space Administration (NASA) to explore space. The "space race" had begun between the United States and the Soviet Union.

Sally was ten years old when John Glenn became the first American to orbit Earth. "I remember the early days of the space program. In elementary school, our teacher rolled in a TV set and we watched some of the first space missions," she said. "It really ignited my interest."[5]

Sally Ride had the same challenge other young people have growing up. What did she want to be? For one thing she enjoyed sports, especially tennis. "When I was a girl, I wanted to be either a professional tennis player, or a scientist. . . . I thought maybe an astronomer.[6] For as long as I can remember I was interested in space, interested in the planets."[7]

▶ Tennis in Her Future

Sally was a gifted athlete. She spent many hours playing baseball with the neighborhood boys. When she turned her attention to tennis, her ability and competitive spirit soon began to show. Sally became good at tennis, and she was ranked eighteenth in the nation in her age group as an amateur player. In 1961, she began taking tennis lessons with four-time national champion Alice Marble.[8] Because of her skill, she earned a scholarship to Westlake School for Girls in Los Angeles. This was a private girls' high school, and Sally became captain of her tennis team in her senior year.[9]

Sally also had another influence. "In high school, I had two teachers who spent a lot of time with me. But more than that, they encouraged me and gave me confidence," she said.[10] After graduation in 1968, Sally attended Swarthmore College. She left school to pursue a career in professional tennis. Eventually Sally decided she did not think she would be a successful tennis pro. Her sister thinks it was because she did not have the "killer

◀ As a young girl, Sally played football and baseball with the boys in her neighborhood. Although she dreamed of one day playing for the Los Angeles Dodgers, her favorite baseball team, Sally was particularly good at tennis.

instinct" needed in professional sports.[11] Her mother said, "She stopped playing tennis because she couldn't make the ball go just where she wanted it to."[12] Sally quit tennis and enrolled at Stanford University.

▶ Answering an Ad

By the age of twenty-seven, Sally Ride had B.A., B.S., and master's degrees, and she was a Ph.D. candidate. That meant she was studying to earn a doctorate degree. One day in 1977, she answered a Stanford University newspaper ad placed by NASA. They were looking for young scientists to serve as "mission specialists" on future space flights. More than eight thousand men and women applied. After a long process of evaluation, thirty-five were accepted. For the first time, six talented women were among them. Judith Resnik had a Ph.D. in electrical engineering. Kathryn Sullivan had a Ph.D. in geology. Anna Fisher and Rhea Seddon were medical doctors. Shannon Lucid was a biochemist.

A NASA press release said, "We have selected an outstanding group of women and men who represent the most competent, talented and experienced people available to us today."[13] This group of astronauts was different from previous groups. They were men and women from diverse ethnic and science backgrounds. NASA's objective was no longer to put a person in space. Now, groups of people would work in space. "My father was probably the happiest person in the world when I was selected as an astronaut," Ride said. "He had a great deal of difficulty explaining what I did when I was an astrophysicist, but when I became an astronaut, his problems were over."[14]

Earlier Space Flights—No Room for Women

Six months after NASA had been created in 1958, the first seven male astronauts were chosen. President Eisenhower had said they must be military test pilots. At the time, there were no female military pilots. Christopher Kraft, former director of the Johnson Space Center, explained, "There were no women in the beginning because they didn't meet the requirements. The men were all test pilots. They were used to life and death situations and put their lives on the line every day."[15] Women objected. They knew they were as good as the men and could handle the challenges of space flight.

First Woman in Space

The Soviet Union did not have the same attitude. In June 1963, Valentina Tereshkova flew into space aboard *Vostok 6*. She remained in space for nearly three days and orbited Earth forty-eight times. On that one flight, she became the first woman in space and the first woman in orbit. Tereshkova was the first person recruited without experience as a test pilot. Her selection was based on her parachuting skills. At the time, Soviet cosmonauts would parachute from the capsule as it returned to Earth.

Mercury 13

During this period, NASA conducted a secret experiment to see if women were candidates for space travel. NASA tested one woman, an aerobatic pilot named Betty Skelton. Her positive results led them to test more female applicants. Eventually twelve other women passed all the tests given to the male astronauts. Originally called First Lady Astronaut Trainees (FLATS), they are now called the

"Mercury 13."[16] NASA did not expect the women to pass the tests, and as a result they did not know what to do with them. Then, NASA decided that they did not want to put women at risk on space flights. After hearings in the U.S. Congress, NASA ended the testing of women for the space program. It would be twenty-two years before American women would fly into space.

▲ Although there were women in NASA's astronaut class of 1978, the class named itself the Thirty-Five New Guys (TFNG). The six female classmates were (left to right) Margaret R. Seddon, Kathryn D. Sullivan, Judith A. Resnik, Sally K. Ride, Anna L. Fisher, and Shannon W. Lucid.

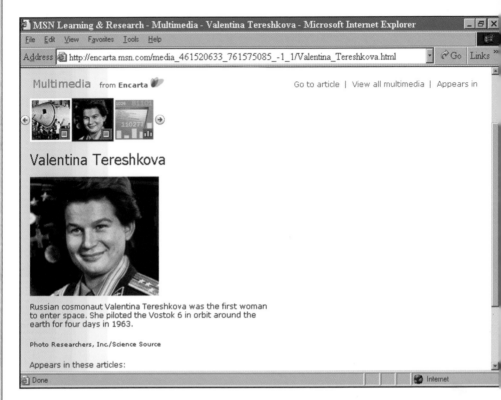

Valentina Tereshkova

Russian cosmonaut Valentina Tereshkova was the first woman to enter space. She piloted the Vostok 6 in orbit around the earth for four days in 1963.

Photo Researchers, Inc./Science Source

Appears in these articles:

Soviet cosmonaut Valentina Tereshkova became the first woman in space in June 1963.

The women's movement of the 1970s also helped to the change attitudes about what women were capable of. At that time, women began to get the opportunity to excel in a variety of fields. Then, in the 1980s, the space shuttle was created. As opposed to space orbiters of the 1960s and 1970s, the shuttles provided some room for personal privacy. Now, women and men could be on the same space ship, and not have to do personal things right in front of one another. These were just a couple reasons why NASA decided it was now time to use women and their talents in space.

TRAINING

"**A**stronaut training is so rigorous that you quickly realize how dangerous this is," says Howard McCurdy, a NASA historian. "Even though you might not be frightened, you are certainly aware of all the other ways things can go." However, the astronauts appear to be fearless. Sally Ride said, "I just want to fly in outer space."[1]

Sally Ride became an astronaut candidate in January 1978. She would train for one year to qualify as an astronaut. To become an astronaut, a person must either be a test pilot, a scientist, or an engineer. Sally Ride was a scientist, with a Ph.D. in physics.

▶ Astronaut Training

The shuttle commander and pilot must train for months so they can fly the shuttle perfectly. Mission specialists must also train and know their jobs well.

Astronaut training is physically and mentally challenging. The program included such things as being dragged behind a motorboat and learning how to eject from an aircraft. After completing her training, Sally Ride would be able to parachute through trees. She would scuba dive in cold water and be lifted by helicopter from a bobbing raft in the ocean. She also learned how to survive in the wilderness. These skills were necessary in case she and the crew had to bail out of the shuttle or make an emergency landing.

▲ In order to become an astronaut, Sally Ride had to hang from a parachute for long periods of time. This was just one of the many grueling training exercises.

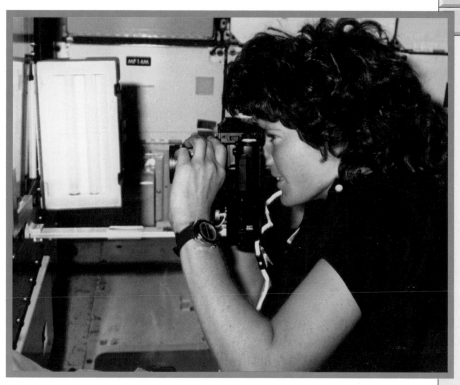

▲ Sally Ride used a camera as part of an experiment she conducted on the space shuttle.

In space, there are tough physical and mental challenges. In the absence of gravity, muscles weaken, including the heart muscle. Astronauts must be in excellent physical condition. Ride was athletic; she ran several miles a day, lifted weights, and played volleyball and tennis. Still, this was new for her.

Ride's training was the same as the men receive. Still, there were some equipment changes because of the gender differences. Some of the women were shorter than the men. Ride was five-feet five-inches tall. NASA redesigned the shuttle seats so they were adjustable, like a car seat.[2]

▲ *As part of her first year of training for NASA, Ride spent about fifteen hours a week in a T-38 training jet. From the backseat of the jet, she learned about navigation and radio communications. She was also able to become more comfortable with different levels of g-forces.*

One of the training exercises simulated microgravity. Gravity is what keeps our feet on the ground. Anytime we drop or throw something, we are watching gravity in action. We believe gravity causes plants to root into the ground. In low-earth orbit, gravity is only a small fraction of that on Earth. This is called microgravity, or "zero g." Sometimes it is called weightlessness. Microgravity describes this very weak gravitational effect.

One way NASA simulates microgravity is by using a KC-135 aircraft. Ride would experience microgravity in this jet nicknamed the "vomit comet." The airplane would climb to about thirty-six thousand feet and then suddenly

Tools   Search   Notes   Discuss

dive toward Earth in a large parabolic arc. The pilot flies these arcs, or half circles, by pulling the nose up to a forty-five-degree angle until the plane will climb no higher. At the top of arc, Ride experienced about two gs. Over the top of the arc, the pilot pushes the stick forward and continues to pitch over until the airplane is forty-five degrees nose down. This will cause the people inside to free fall, becoming nearly weightless. These simulations last about twenty-five seconds. During a flight, which lasts about two hours, the crew may fly forty arcs. Ride and the others experienced about thirteen minutes of microgravity. This experience sometimes has a yucky result. Some people get very ill. That is why the plane is called the "vomit comet." Ride, though, never got sick.

Advanced Training

After Sally Ride completed her training, she was eligible for assignment as a mission specialist on a future space shuttle flight. A mission specialist is not a pilot. He or she is responsible for coordinating onboard operations. Mission specialists perform onboard experiments and may make spacewalks.

Ride also went through additional training. Some of this training involved different courses including guidance, navigation, and payload deployment. There were hours of classroom lectures about computer science, engineering, and physics.

Even though Ride had successfully completed astronaut training, she was not yet ready to fly a shuttle mission. There was also a list of astronauts waiting for their chance to go into space. One astronaut, Deke Slayton, waited fourteen years to fly into space because of an illness.[3]

▲ *Sally Ride was the first female CAPCOM. The CAPCOM speaks to the shuttle crew from Mission Control.*

While waiting for an assignment, all astronauts work at the Shuttle Avionics Integration Laboratory (SAIL). Like all new astronauts, Ride needed experience working in and around the shuttle before she could be assigned to an actual flight. At SAIL, Ride practiced simulated emergencies and other procedures. Astronauts must know everything there is to know about the shuttle. They must know each of the systems much like a doctor knows the inside of the human body. Every system on the shuttle must be memorized and its function understood. With this kind of training, NASA hopes that the astronauts will develop quick reflexes. If there is an emergency during a flight, they will not have to think about what to do. They will react with the correct response immediately.

When there is a shuttle mission, the new astronauts become part of Mission Control. They will support the mission astronauts. Ride's job during the second and third flights of *Columbia* was to serve in the important role of capsule, or ground communications officer (CAPCOM). The CAPCOM is the only person who talks to the shuttle crew from the ground. He or she relays information from the flight director and answers questions the crew may have. The CAPCOM has to be calm under pressure. Ride was the first woman to have this responsibility.

Training continued even after Ride had a flight assignment. About ten weeks before the mission, the astronauts begin to simulate the mission with the Mission Control team. These simulations permit the crew and Mission Control to practice operating as a team.

While at NASA, Ride met another astronaut trainee, Dr. Steven Hawley. They quietly married in 1982. Ride, who had earned her pilot's license in training, flew to her wedding. Afterwards, she flew her new husband to their honeymoon.[4]

▶ Unwanted Publicity

When NASA announced that Sally Ride would become the first American woman they would send into space, she became an instant celebrity. Newspapers, magazines, and television shows interviewed her. She did not like the publicity and tried to avoid questions from the press. "She doesn't offer information," said her sister, Karen, "if you want to know something about Sally, you have to ask her."[5] When reporters did, they seemed to ask the wrong

questions. They asked her for personal information such as whether she would take lipstick or perfume along. One reporter asked if she "weeps" when she has a problem. Ride was quick to reply, "Why doesn't someone ask Rick?" (the pilot).[6] "It's too bad," she said, "that society isn't to the point yet where the country could just send up a woman astronaut and nobody would think twice about it."[7] Ride was so popular that singer Casse Culver wrote a song about her: "Ride Sally ride, ride that big bird in the sky."[8]

Flight director John Cox said, "She showed that she's just as capable as any of the men."[9] Not everyone was convinced. Astronaut Alan Beam questioned whether women could tackle such "male things" as spacecraft and computers.[10] He did not know Sally Ride. She had spent hours in front of a computer in graduate school. He later changed his mind and agreed women performed as well as men.[11]

Women had climbed the highest mountains and dived the depths of the oceans. Now a woman was on her way to space, the final frontier.

IN ORBIT

Although not the pilot on the shuttle, Ride had specific duties during liftoff and landing. She sat behind the commander and the pilot and served as the flight engineer. Her job was to monitor data from the instrument panel. In an emergency, she would suggest corrective action.

▶ Satellite Doctors

Five days into the flight, it was time for Ride's main responsibility to begin. She would operate the shuttle's

▲ Sally Ride served as the mission specialist aboard *Challenger*. Part of her job included monitoring control panels and calling out data to the pilot and commander.

fifty-foot mechanical arm, called the remote manipulator system (RMS). The cherrypicker-like device would play an important role in the shuttle's future. The device was placed in the shuttle's cargo bay. First, Ride would use the RMS to lift a special item (called a payload) out of the cargo bay. Then, she would toss the item into space. Next, she would capture the item and place it back into the cargo bay. The experiment was to test the shuttle crew's ability to capture broken satellites, repair them, or bring them back to Earth. Ride was successful. During the mission, the crew also released satellites for Canada and Indonesia.

The crew performed about forty scientific experiments. Some included observing how small plants grow in zero gravity. One experiment came from a group of high school students in New Jersey. They had sent a colony of carpenter ants. The students wanted the astronauts to observe how weightlessness affected the way the ants behaved.

One important experiment was to test a procedure that might shorten the preparation time for an astronaut going to walk in space. Astronauts had to breathe pure oxygen for three hours before making a spacewalk. The experiment would see if this time could be reduced. The test was conducted while the crew was asleep. They reduced the cabin pressure and regulated the mix of oxygen and nitrogen. The experiment was successful, and new procedures were used on future spacewalks.

▶ The Crew

The crew was handpicked because each had a special talent needed for the success of the mission. Commander Robert L. Crippen served as a pilot aboard an aircraft carrier. He logged more than 6,500 hours of flying time. He was the pilot on *Columbia*'s first test flight in April 1981. Crippen

Astronaut Bio: Robert L. Crippen - Microsoft Internet Explorer

File Edit View Favorites Tools Help

Address http://vesuvius.jsc.nasa.gov/Bios/htmlbios/crippen-rl.html   Go Links

Biographical Data

Lyndon B. Johnson Space Center
Houston, Texas 77058

National Aeronautics and
Space Administration

NAME: Robert L. Crippen (Captain, USN, Ret.)
NASA Astronaut (former)

PERSONAL DATA: Born in Beaumont, Texas, on September 11, 1937. Married to
the former Pandora Lee Puckett of Miami, Florida. Three grown daughters.

EDUCATION: Graduated from New Caney High School in Caney, Texas; received a
bachelor of science degree in Aerospace Engineering from the University of Texas in
1960.

ORGANIZATIONS: Fellow, American Institute of Aeronautics and Astronautics;
American Astronautical Society; and Society of Experimental Test Pilots.

SPECIAL HONORS: NASA Outstanding Leadership Medal (1988); Distinguished
Service Medals (1985, 1988, 1993); U.S. Navy Distinguished Flying Cross (1984); Defense Meritorious Service Medal
(1984); Federal Aviation Administration's Award for Distinguished Service (1982), Goddard Memorial Trophy (1982),
Harmon Trophy (1982); NASA Space Flight Medals (1981, 1983, and 2 in 1984); NASA Distinguished Service Medal

Internet

 *Commander Robert L. Crippen picked Ride as one of the mission specialists because she was an excellent engineer that worked well under stress. He also felt that her personality would fit well with the rest of the crew.*

picked Ride as a mission specialist because she could remain calm under pressure. President Reagan had said she was "the best person for the job."[1]

Frederick (Rick) H. Hauck was the shuttle's pilot. He flew Navy combat missions and later served as a test pilot. Hauck later became commander for the second mission of the space shuttle *Discovery* in November 1984. He was also commander of *Discovery* on the first flight after the *Challenger* accident.

Mission specialist John M. Fabian was an Air Force combat pilot. He logged four thousand hours of flying time. This was his first space flight.

Doctor Norman E. Thagard was the first American medical doctor in space. Thagard, also referred to as a mission specialist, flew combat missions in Vietnam. His job was to try to discover why some astronauts got space sickness.[2]

▶ Life On Board the Shuttle

There is no air to breathe or water to drink in space. However, the space shuttle is pressurized and provides air and temperatures needed to survive in space. The atmosphere in the cabin is like inside an airliner. Ride and the other crew ate specially prepared, precooked, and dried meals. Water was added to the plastic pouches to moisten the food. There was enough water for washing and drinking since it was a by-product of the shuttle's fuel cells.

Even though engineers had tried to make the environment as close to Earth as possible, Ride and the crew had some adjustments to make. The shuttle had a personal hygiene station where the crew could wash, brush their teeth, and use the toilet. There was a curtain for privacy. The toilet was similar to one in an airliner except it had foot restraints and a seat belt. Instead of the bio-wastes being flushed away with water, they were swept away with suction. These wastes are not dumped overboard but are dried and stored for removal when the shuttle lands.

There are no beds on board the shuttle. The crew uses sleeping bags to restrain themselves when they sleep.[3] This is necessary to avoid floating around. Cabin fans circulate air inside the crew compartment. If the astronauts were free-floating, they might float with the air current and bump into each other or accidentally bump into switches.

Each crew member also has a personal sleep kit. It contains eyeshades and earplugs. These will shut out light and noises from the fans, pumps, and equipment inside the shuttle.

Doctors knew that exercise in space was important to preventing bone density loss. One of the exercises Ride did was run on a treadmill. Later she joked that she was "probably one of the few people to run across the Indian Ocean."[4] She had been using the treadmill as the shuttle passed over it.

Eating in space was a challenge. It involved attaching the food pouch to a tray with Velcro. Ride would strap the tray to her leg, and the crew could eat picnic-style, while floating around the cabin. They could also attach the trays to a special table.

Cleaning up was very important. Scientists found that microbes, or germs, grew very fast in microgravity. To prevent this, Ride and the crew wiped the surfaces clean with cloths containing a germ-killing liquid.

If astronauts did not have sleeping bags to stop them from floating around the shuttle, they might bump into each other and the machinery.

▶ Return to Earth

Ride's first flight lasted about six days. She orbited Earth ninety-seven times and traveled 2.2 million miles. "Probably the most spectacular part is when you begin re-entering Earth's atmosphere," she said. "The shuttle is just screaming down, so it, it's ionizing the atmosphere. That's usually done in the dark on the night side of the planet if the landing is going to be in the daylight. That happens . . . when you come down to about 400,000 feet," she said. "When you look out the windows, all you see is orange and pink glow, seemingly surrounding the shuttle—almost looks like flames licking the shuttle."[5]

The shuttle was due to land in Florida, but because of bad weather, it landed in California. A small crowd greeted the astronauts when they landed. One sign recognized Ride's history-making flight. It proclaimed, "Herstory made today by Sally Ride."[6]

When the crew returned, Ride was asked many questions. She even had offers from Hollywood agents who wanted her to appear on television or in the movies. Her response to some of the questions was, "I didn't come into the space program to be the first woman in space. I came into it to get a chance to fly as soon as I could."[7]

After the flight, Ride remarked about how she and her fellow crew members got along. "The thing that I'll remember most about the flight is that it was fun. In fact, I'm sure it was the most fun that I will ever have in my life."[8]

▶ Ride's Second Voyage into Space

After her historic flight, Ride told reporters, "I'd love to go into space again. I just wouldn't want to go through training!"[9] The lure of space was strong for Ride. She went through the training again, and in October 1984, Ride

Astronaut Bio: John M. Fabian - Microsoft Internet Explorer

File   Edit   View   Favorites   Tools   Help

Address   http://www.jsc.nasa.gov/Bios/htmlbios/fabian-jm.html   Go   Links

Biographical Data

Lyndon B. Johnson Space Center
Houston, Texas 77058

National Aeronautics and
Space Administration

NAME: John M. Fabian (Colonel, USAF, Ret.)
     NASA Astronaut (former)

PERSONAL DATA: Born January 28, 1939, in Goosecreek, Texas, but considers Pullman, Washington, to be his hometown. Married to the former, Donna Kay Buboltz of Spokane, Washington. They have two grown children. Recreational interests include skiing, stamp collecting, and jogging.

EDUCATION: Graduated from Pullman High School, Pullman, Washington, in 1957; received a bachelor of science degree in Mechanical Engineering from Washington State University in 1962; a master of science in Aerospace Engineering from the Air Force Institute of Technology in 1964; and a doctorate in Aeronautics and Astronautics from the University of Washington in 1974.

ORGANIZATIONS: Associate Fellow, American Institute of Aeronautics and Astronautics; Fellow, American Astronautical Society; President, Association of Space Explorers; Corresponding Member, International Academy of Astronautics.

Internet

Like Sally Ride, John Fabian was a mission specialist aboard Challenger *STS-7. Ride and Fabian worked very closely. Using a remote manipulator arm, they became the first people to retrieve a satellite in space.*

served as a mission specialist on the space shuttle *Challenger* once again. This time it was the thirteenth shuttle flight. By now, the novelty of a woman in space had worn off. Dr. Judith Resnik had flown aboard *Discovery* in 1984. Among the seven people on board the second flight was another woman, Dr. Kathryn D. Sullivan. The seven-person crew made it the largest crew to fly to date. During their eight-day mission, the crew released a satellite and conducted scientific observations

http://science.ksc.nasa.gov/shuttle/missions/sts-7/sts-7-patch.jpg - Microsoft Internet Explorer

File   Edit   View   Favorites   Tools   Help

Address   http://science.ksc.nasa.gov/shuttle/missions/sts-7/sts-7-patch.jpg   Go   Links

▲ *This is the mission patch that the astronauts wore on Ride's first space flight.*

of Earth. The mission ended with a landing at the Kennedy Space Center in Florida.

In June 1985, Ride was assigned to a third space shuttle flight. Training for that flight was suspended when *Challenger* blew up during launch on January 28, 1986. For the next six months, Ride served as a member of the Presidential Commission investigating the *Challenger* accident.

WOMEN IN SPACE— THE LEGACY

Investigating the cause of the *Challenger* accident was difficult for Sally Ride. She had known the *Challenger* crew. They had been her friends. A television reporter asked if she and her fellow astronauts were ready to fly again. Ride said, "I am not ready to fly again. I think there are very few astronauts who are ready to fly again now. . . . We may have been misleading people into thinking that this is a routine operation, that it's just like getting on an airliner and going across the country and that it's safe. And it's not."

Sally Ride reminded Americans how dangerous space flight was. "Rocket technology is risky," she said, "and those risks are something that every astronaut has to internally come to grips with and be willing to accept."[1] Eventually, the board found the cause of the *Challenger* accident and took steps to prevent it from happening again.

Later, Ride went to work as assistant to the administrator for long-range planning, in Washington. In this role she created NASA's Office of Exploration and produced a report on the future of the space program called "Leadership and America's Future in Space."

The work became known as the "Ride Report." It had four options for NASA, after the International Space Station was assembled. It included "Mission Earth," a study of earth sciences using satellite sensors; exploration of remote parts of the solar system; and an expedition to Mars.

▲ *Sally Ride created Imaginary Lines, Inc. Imaginary Lines encourages girls to explore their interests in science and technology by providing different programs and products.*

Ride's report also recommended building a permanent moon base.[2]

▷ Later Accomplishments

Sally Ride left NASA in 1987 to become a Science Fellow at the Center for International Security and Arms Control at Stanford University. After two years, she was named director of the California Space Institute and professor of physics at the University of California, San Diego.

In 1994, Dr. Sally Ride started EarthKAM. Her goal was to integrate education with the space program. In addition, Ride is the author of five children's books. *To Space and Back*, describes her experiences in space. She also wrote *Voyager: An Adventure to the Edge of the Solar System, The Third Planet: Exploring the Earth from Space, Exploring Our Solar System,* and *The Mystery of Mars.* Ride has received numerous awards, including the Jefferson Award for Public Service, the Women's Research and Education Institute's American Woman Award, and has been twice awarded the National Space flight Medal.

▶ Imaginary Lines

Ride knew that in elementary school, girls and boys are often equally interested in math, science, and computers.

▲ *Kathryn D. Sullivan (left) and Sally Ride show off a sleeping restraint that astronauts call "a bag of worms" because of all of the small tubes sticking out of it.*

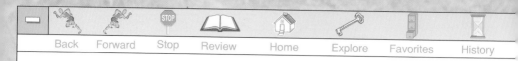

△ By the end of 2003, a total of forty-one women had the opportunity
to fly in space.

"If you ask third graders whether they're interested in science,
just as many girls as boys will raise their hands. But some-
where in the fourth, fifth or sixth grade, girls start to drift
away," said Ride.[3] That is why Ride formed "Imaginary
Lines," a company to encourage young girls to become
interested in science and technology. The Sally Ride Science
Club encourages girls in the fourth through eighth grades
to explore fields of science. The club holds science fairs,
provides mentors, and publishes a newsletter.

Tools   Search   Notes   Discuss   Go!

▲ Sally Ride has had a great deal of influence over the space program in the United States, including paving the way for future female astronauts. Now she hopes to continue this influence through her teaching and many programs for America's youth.

Sally Ride Space Camp

Sally Ride was aware that young girls did not get the same opportunities as young boys in the areas of science and technology. So she created the Sally Ride Space Camp for girls between seven and eleven years of age. "Everywhere I go, I run into girls who've been to space camp and want to become astronauts. . . . I would love to see those same stars in their eyes in ten or fifteen years and know they're on their way," she said.[4]

Columbia Accident

On February 1, 2003, tragedy struck the space shuttle *Columbia.* Sixteen minutes from a landing, it broke apart in flight. All seven crew members died. Ride was appointed to the board investigating the accident.

▲ Although Sally Ride left NASA in the 1980s, she was chosen to help investigate the cause of the Columbia accident.

"We'll pick up the torch the astronauts carried and carry it forward," she said. "I think that although yesterday really was a horrible day for the space program, the space program will go on, it will continue and it will be better than it is today," she said.[5]

▶ Women in Space Today

Since Sally Ride's historic flight, dozens of women have flown into space and returned. Four have given their lives in the quest for knowledge. Today, NASA provides women with equal treatment and opportunity. For example, Colonel Eileen Collins has become space shuttle pilot and commander.

Speaking before a group of young girls, Ride described her two space flights aboard the shuttle *Challenger*. "When I was a little girl, I dreamed of flying in space. Amazingly, enough, and I still can't believe it, that dream came true. And through hard work and a good education, all of you will reach for the stars and that dream will come true for you."[6]

Sally Ride is an American hero and a role model. She believes women can do anything, and her actions prove she is right.

Chapter 2. Growing Up

1. "Astronaut Sally Ride Works to Bridge Gender Gap in Science, Math." *San Francisco Chronicle*, November 24, 2002, <http://www.sfgate.com/cgibin/article.cgi?f=/news/archive/2002/11/24/state0006EST0133.DTL> (May 7, 2003).

2. "Sally Ride Breaks the Space Barrier," *McCalls*, June 1983, p. 60.

3. Frederic Golden, "Sally's Joy Ride into the Sky," *Time*, June 13, 1983, p. 57.

4. Laura S. Woodmansee, *Women Astronauts* (Ontario, Canada: Apogee Books, 2002), p. 52.

5. John Tylko, "Sally Ride tells girls about career as astronaut at MIT event," *TechTalk*, September 25, 2002, <http://web.mit.edu/newsoffice/tt/2002/sep25/sally.html> (December 8, 2003).

6. Woodmansee, p. 53.

7. Ibid., p. 52.

8. Cislunar Aerospace, "The Right Stuff—On and Off the Court," *Feature Presentation*, 1997, <http://wings.avkids.com/Tennis/Features/ride-01.html> (December 8, 2003).

9. Ibid.

10. "Astronaut Sally Ride Works to Bridge Gender Gap in Science, Math." *San Francisco Chronicle*, November 24, 2002, <http://www.sfgate.com/cgibin/article.cgi?f=/news/archive/2002/11/24/state0006EST0133.DTL> (May 29, 2003).

11. Jerry Adler and Pamela Abramson, "Sally Ride: Ready for Liftoff," *Newsweek*, June 13, 1983, p. 40.

12. Ibid.

13. Woodmansee, p. 40.

14. Tylko, "Sally Ride tells girls about career as astronaut at MIT event."

15. Golden, p. 56.

16. Woodmansee, p. 27.

Chapter 3. Training

1. Wellington, New Zealand, Ministry of Education,

"The Columbia and the NASA Shuttle Programme," *TKI Hot Topic*, 2003, <http://www.tki.org.nz/r/hot_topics/columbia_e.php> (December 8, 2003).

2. Frederic Golden, "Sally's Joy Ride into the Sky," *Time*, June 13, 1983, p. 57.

3. Tara Gray , "Donald K. "Deke" Slayton," *Anniversary of the Mercury 7*, n.d., <http://history.nasa.gov/40thmerc7/slayton.htm> (December 8, 2003).

4. Peter Bond, *Heroes in Space: From Gagarin to Challenger* (Malden, Mass.: Basil Blackwell, Inc., 1987), p. 409.

5. Jerry Adler and Pamela Abramson, "Sally Ride: Ready for Liftoff," *Newsweek*, June 13, 1983, p. 38.

6. Ibid., pp. 39–40.

7. Golden, p. 56.

8. Frederic Golden, "Toward the New Frontier," *Time*, June 27, 1983, p. 12.

9. Frederic Golden, "Mission Accomplished," *Time*, July 4, 1983, p. 26.

10. Frederic Golden, "Sally's Joy Ride into the Sky," p. 57.

11. Ibid.

Chapter 4. In Orbit

1. Frederic Golden, Mission Accomplished, *Time*, July 4, 1983, p. 26.

2. Peter Bond, *Heroes in Space: From Gagarin to Challenger* (Malden, Mass.: Basil Blackwell, Inc., 1987), p. 410.

3. Judith L. Robinson, Ph.D., "Sleeping on Board the Space Shuttle," *NASA Neurolab Web*, February 28, 2002, <http://lsda.jsc.nasa.gov/kids/L&W/sleep.htm> (December 8, 2003).

4. Sharon Begley, et. al., "Challenger's Happy Landing," *Newsweek*, July 4, 1983, p. 70.

5. ABCNEWS Internet Ventures, "Shuttle Landing Usually Quite a Ride," February 3, 2003, <http://abcnews.go.com/sections/scitech/DailyNews/shuttle_ride030202.html> (December 8, 2003).

6. Begley, et. al., p. 68.

7. Frederic Golden, "Sally's Joy Ride into the Sky," *Time*, June 13, 1983, p. 56.

8. Begley, et. al., p. 68.

9. Laura S. Woodmansee, *Women Astronauts* (Ontario, Canada: Apogee Books, 2002), p. 41.

Chapter 5. Women in Space—The Legacy

1. Laura S. Woodmansee, *Women Astronauts* (Ontario, Canada: Apogee Books, 2002), p. 44.

2. Mark Carreau, "Sally Ride is Leaving NASA After Making Major Contributions," September 21, 1987, <http://www.chron.com/content/interactive/space/archives/87/870921.html> (December 8, 2003).

3. Susan Korones Gifford, "An Astronaut's Amazing Mission," *Good Housekeeping*, November 2001, p. 98.

4. Ibid.

5. The Associated Press, "U.S. Tries to Move on From Space Tragedy," February 2, 2003, <http://abcnews.go.com/wire/US/ap20030202_1659.html#photocap> (December 8, 2003).

6. John Tylko, "Sally Ride tells girls about career as astronaut at MIT event," *TechTalk*, September 25, 2002, <http://web.mit.edu/newsoffice/tt/2002/sep25/sally.html> (December 8, 2003).

Further Reading

Books

Gomez, Rebecca. *Sally Ride.* Edina, Minn.: ABDO Publishing Company, 2003.

Kramer, Barbara. *Sally Ride: A Space Biography.* Springfield, N.J.: Enslow Publishers, Inc., 1998.

Orr, Tamra. *Sally Ride: The First American Woman in Space.* New York: The Rosen Publishing Group, 2003.

Pasternak, Ceel, and Linda Thornburg. *Cool Careers for Girls in Air and Space.* Manassas Park, Va.: Impact Publications, 2001.

Ride, Sally, with Tam O'Shaughnessy. *Exploring Our Solar System.* New York: Crown Publishers, 2003.

————— , *The Mystery of Mars.* New York: Random House Children's Books, 1999.

Wade, Linda R. *Sally Ride: The Story of the First American Female in Space.* Bear, Del.: Mitchell Lane Publishers, 2002.

Video

Women In Space. K. R. Carrington Productions. Venice, Calif.: TMW Media Group, Inc., 2000. (Interview with Sally Ride, et al.)

Back	Forward	Stop	Review	Home	Explore	Favorites	History

Index